Look After Yourself
Get Some Rest!

Angela Royston

Heinemann LIBRARY

H **www.heinemann.co.uk/library**
Visit our website to find out more information about **Heinemann Library** books.

To order:
☎ Phone 44 (0) 1865 888066
🖹 Send a fax to 44 (0) 1865 314091
🖥 Visit the Heinemann Bookshop at www.heinemann.co.uk/library to browse our catalogue and order online.

First published in Great Britain by Heinemann Library, Halley Court, Jordan Hill, Oxford OX2 8EJ, part of Harcourt Education. Heinemann is a registered trademark of Harcourt Education Ltd.

Editorial: Sarah Eason and Kathy Peltan
Design: Dave Oakley, Arnos Design
Picture Research: Helen Reilly, Arnos Design
Production: Edward Moore

Originated by Dot Gradations Ltd
Printed and bound in Hong Kong and China by South China

ISBN 0 431 18021 0
07 06 05 04 03
10 9 8 7 6 5 4 3 2 1

British Library Cataloguing in Publication Data
Royston, Angela
Get some rest. – (Look after yourself)
1.Rest – Juvenile literature
I.Title
613.7'9

A full catalogue record for this book is available from the British Library.

Acknowledgements
The publishers would like to thank the following for permission to reproduce photographs: Bubbles p.**5** (Lucy Tizard) p.**9** (Frans Rombout), p.**25** (Ian West); Getty Images p.**11** (Peter Hince), p.**13** (David Roth), p.**16** White Packert); Last Resort p.**24** (Jo Makin); Photodisc pp.**10**, **21**, **26**; Powerstock pp.**4**, **8**; Science Photo Library p.**14** (Gaillard, Jerrican), p.**20** (Mark Clarke); Trevor Clifford pp.**6**, **7**, **15**, **18**, **19**, **22**, **23**, **27**; Trip p.**12** (S. Grant), p.**17** (S. Grant).

Cover photograph reproduced with permission of SuperStock/Kwame Zikomo.

The publishers would like to thank David Wright for his assistance in the preparation of this book.

Every effort has been made to contact copyright holders of any material reproduced in this book. Any omissions will be rectified in subsequent printings if notice is given to the publishers.

Contents

Words written in bold, **like this**, are explained in the Glossary.

Your body

Your body is made up of many different parts that work together. You use the **muscles** in your arms and legs to make a swing go higher and faster.

When you have been doing something **energetic**, you may feel tired. This book tells you how resting your mind and your body will help you to stay healthy.

You need to rest

Exercise is good for your body, but you also need to rest. After you have been running fast you often feel tired and **out of breath**.

Your **muscles** have been working hard, and so have your **heart** and **lungs**. Try sitting down for a few minutes to let these parts of your body recover.

Relax after exercise

Climbing and walking uses lots of **energy**. It can make your body very tired. It can also make the **muscles** in your legs ache.

After exercise, you may feel too tired to move and just want to rest. Playing a quiet game is one way to rest your body.

Relax after thinking

Sometimes your **brain** needs to **relax**.
When you work hard at school, you have to
concentrate. You use your brain to think,
and thinking makes you tired.

After a while, your brain needs a rest. At school you have breaks when you can go outside. Playing is a good way to rest your brain.

Sleep

When you go to sleep at night, you rest your body and your **brain**. Your **muscles** rest. Your brain does not have to **concentrate** or think.

Other parts of your body slow down when you sleep. Your **heart** beats more slowly. You breathe more deeply. When you wake up, your whole body feels rested and full of **energy**.

Get enough sleep

If you do not get enough sleep, you will wake up feeling tired. You might also become tired during the day. It is harder to learn when you are tired.

If you are very tired, you will easily become cross. You may not enjoy playing with your friends. Children need to sleep for about 10 hours every night.

Many children have a bath before they go to bed. The hot water helps them to **relax**, and the bath becomes a **routine**. Doing the same thing every night helps you get to sleep.

16

You are more likely to fall asleep if you are relaxed. Reading a story before you go to sleep is a good way to relax. Listening to music is relaxing too.

Go to bed at the same time every night

You sleep better if you go to bed at about the same time every night. Your body gets used to going to sleep at that time.

18

Most people also wake up at about the same time every morning. If you have slept for long enough, you will find it easy to wake up.

Avoid getting overtired

Make sure you go to bed early enough. Many children try to put off going to bed. But when you are tired you can easily become upset.

20

If you stay up late, your **brain** is awake for too long. You become **overtired**. It is harder to get to sleep when you are overtired.

Broken sleep

You probably wake up in the middle of the night sometimes. Some people wake up because they have a cough. Or you may need to go to the toilet.

You may wake up because you are thirsty. Keep a glass of water beside your bed. A drink of water will help you get back to sleep.

Night time terrors

Most people sleep better in a dark room. Sometimes ordinary things can look scary in the dark. A night light is dim but it lets you see things properly.

Everyone has bad dreams from time to time.
Bad dreams can make you feel scared.
Sometimes you need an adult to tell you that
your dreams are not real.

Extra rest

When you are ill, you usually sleep for longer. Sometimes you may stay asleep all day. Your body is using lots of **energy** to fight the illness. This will make you feel tired.

When you get a bit better, you may want to sit up. Even then you need to sit still and rest. Resting helps your body to get well more quickly.

27

Avoid eating a large meal just before you go to bed. Your body cannot **digest** food very well when you are asleep. You may get **indigestion** and this can give you bad dreams.

Feeling hungry can keep you awake at night. It is best to eat the last meal of the day three or four hours before you go to bed. A small **snack** just before bedtime can help you sleep.

A warm drink can also help you get to sleep. A drink of warm milk, hot chocolate or **camomile** tea can make you feel relaxed and so help you fall asleep.

Avoid drinks that may keep you awake. Cola, tea and coffee all contain a drug called **caffeine**. Caffeine makes your **brain** alert and will stop you sleeping so well.

The first few hours of sleep are the deepest. Most people have three, four or five dreams each night. You only remember a dream if you wake up in the middle of it.

Sleep is important for giving you a healthy mind as well as a healthy body. People who have not slept for more than three days cannot think clearly. They begin to see and hear things that are not there.

Glossary

brain   the part of the body that controls the whole body and allows you to be aware of things

caffeine   drug which makes you feel more awake and alert. Tea, coffee and cola all contain caffeine.

camomile   plant that is made into medicine or into tea that makes you feel calmer

concentrate   think hard about one thing

digest   when your stomach breaks down food after eating

energetic   using lots of energy

energy   the power to do work or move about

exercise   activities that make your muscles work hard

heart   the part of the body that pumps blood around

indigestion   when your stomach or intestines feel swollen or painful after eating

lungs   parts of the body that take in oxygen from the air you breathe in

muscle   part of the body that tightens to move a bone or other part of the body

out of breath   panting or gasping for air

overtired   too tired

relax   rest your body and mind

routine   the way you usually do something

snack   food eaten between meals

Find out more

My Amazing Body: A First Look at Health and Fitness by Pat Thomas and Lesley Harker (Hodder Wayland, 2002)

My Healthy Body: Fit and Well by Veronica Ross (Belitha Press, 2002)

Well Being: Physical Well Being, Sleep by Joy Cowley and Enrico Sallustio (Folens, 2001)

What About Health: Exercise by Fiona Waters (Hodder Wayland, 2001)

Index

Titles in the *Look After Yourself* series include:

Hardback   0 431 18020 2

Hardback   0 431 18021 0

Hardback   0 431 18026 1

Hardback   0 431 18019 9

Hardback   0 431 18025 3

Hardback   0 431 18024 5

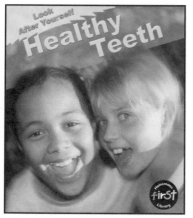

Hardback   0 431 18022 9

Hardback   0 431 18027 X

Find out about the other titles in this series on our website www.heinemann.co.uk/library